500 Awesome Writing Prompts for High School Classrooms

Thought-provoking ideas to get students writing!

Sandra Clair

TABLE OF CONETNETS

INTRODUCTION

500 Awesome Writing Prompts for High School Students is a comprehensive collection of thought-provoking writing prompts for high school classrooms. They can be used in any teaching situation, including classrooms, homeschool, and afterschool programs. They would also be great in literary stations, writing folders, or used as bell ringers or discussion starters. Either way, this awesome collection contains hundreds of prompts in 25 well-organized categories.

With hundreds of compelling and intriguing prompts to choose from, you'll never run out of ideas ever again! Use them with your students to blast through writer's block and get their creative juices flowing! From literature to sports to celebrities to creative writing, there is something here for everyone!

1. Coming of Age

1. Describe a time when you were pressured to make the wrong decision. How has that decision changed you? What lessons have you learned from that experience?
2. Discuss the first time you experienced racism or prejudice in school. What effect has it had on you?
3. Examine a moment that you experienced social injustice from a teacher. This might be where favoritism affected you, or you were punished unfairly.
4. Describe the way a loss has changed your life. It could be a loss of a family member pet or friend.
5. Discuss a fear you have of the unknown. It could be a fear of losing someone, death, or an upcoming event.
6. Examine how you have changed from elementary school until now. How have your choices shaped you or changed the course of your life?
7. Think about your fears and insecurities about school safety. Examine your feelings about school massacres that have happened in the past. How has this changed you? What do you feel when a school goes into lockdown? What do you think when you hear about another school massacre?
8. Examine your feelings about the pressure to have sex. Discuss how it affects you and your friends.

9. Discuss your experiences with teen drinking or drug use. What led to the drinking or drug use? How has it affected you? What advice would you give to other teenagers about alcohol and drugs?

10. Describe how a close friend became an enemy. What led to it? How has it changed you? How did it change them?

11. Describe the feelings of love never realized. Why was it not realized? What effect did it have on you?

12. Write about the feelings of first love. If you haven't had a first love, what are your expectations?

13. Examine the euphoria or awkwardness of your first kiss.

14. Write about the current political climate. How do you feel about it? How does it affect you?

15. How does racism affect your community? Detail a personal experience you've had.

16. Describe how a catastrophic event that has happened in the country or around the world affected you personally.

17. Discuss the epidemic of teen pregnancy and the impact it has on communities

18. Discuss a time you had to deal with racism.

19. Discuss something that you did that challenged or scared you.

20. Describe a time you experienced a breakup. What led to the breakup? How did you feel about it? How do you think about it now?

2. Social Media

1. In what ways may social media help or hurt a person's college or professional goals?
2. Should people be allowed to hide who they are online? Why, or why not?
3. Should what a person writes on social media be the reason for them to get fired?
4. Does social media make people feel more connected or make them feel more alone? Why or why not?
5. Write an analysis of the uses of social media. Provide a review of its strengths and weaknesses.
6. Compare and contrast two different types of social media. For example, compare Instagram to Twitter.
7. How young is too young to use social media? Explain.
8. What are some reasons that someone would consider deleting their Facebook account?
9. Facebook, or Instagram? Which do you prefer? Why?
10. Does social media make some people more narcissistic? Why or why not?
11. Is social media addictive? Explain.
12. How do social media companies exploit their users?

13. What is a positive contribution that social media has had on society at large?
14. How have social media companies failed to protect the privacy of users?
15. What are the advantages and disadvantages of allowing social media in schools?
16. What are some of the unforeseen challenges that social media has created for society?
17. Social media should not be censored in any way. Explain your viewpoint on this statement.
18. How has social media helped in the spread of radical ideas?
19. How does social media contribute to the body image of teenagers?
20. How is social media responsible for the dissemination of false information?

3.Technology

1. Describe a time in your life when technology positively affected you.
2. Describe a time in your life when technology negatively affected you.
3. How has technology changed relationships with people in your life? Cite examples.
4. Which technology do you think has had the most positive impact on society as a whole? Why?
5. Which technology do you think has had the most negative effect on society as a whole? Why?
6. Describe one technology that you feel you could never live without. Why?
7. Imagine for a moment that you were born in a time when gaming, television, movies, and the Internet were never invented. How would you, your friends and family entertain yourselves? Cite examples.
8. Robots will probably be a part of our everyday lives in the future. What are the advantages and disadvantages of having robots in the home?
9. Should parents have access to their children's cell phones? Why or why not?
10. Which do you prefer, a PC or a Mac? Why?

11. What impact will robots have on our future?
12. How will self-driving cars evolve in the future?
13. Would you consider deleting your social media accounts? Why or why not?
14. Which technology do you think will have the most significant impact on the future -either positively or negatively? Why?
15. What new technologies do you think will be invented in the future? Explain.
16. Should the cloning of animals be allowed? Why, or why not?
17. Is online education comparable to face-to-face learning? Why or why not?
18. Does the use of technology in classes benefit the educational process?
19. Should genetically modified foods be banned? Why or why not?
20. What is the role of technology in medicine?

4. Bullying

1. What steps do you think can be taken as a society to put a stop to bullying?
2. What are some stringent punishments that could be imposed on people who bully others?
3. What is the end-result of watching while someone else is bullied?
4. Compare and contrast the mental and physiological impact of bullying on the person being bullied and the person doing the bullying.
5. Describe some intervention and prevention initiatives that can be used to prevent bullying in schools.
6. Explain some reasons why society may never be able to put an end to bullying.
7. Discuss the different manifestations of bullying.
8. How might bullying evolve over the next 50 years? Will it get worse, or will it get better?
9. What can governments do to end bullying in a society?
10. Some people say that bullying is a natural part of growing up. Others believe it's unnatural and should be prevented at all costs. Discuss.
11. What are some ways to stop someone from bullying another person?
12. Compare and contrast the difference between bullying and teasing.

13. Are there particular types of attitudes that contribute to someone being a bully? Explain.

14. Describe a time you stood up for something you believed in.

15. What are the risks of standing up to a bully? Explain.

16. Do you think that bullying should be criminalized? Why or why not?

17. From your experience, is bullying more prevalent between girls or between boys? Explain.

18. Discuss the effectiveness of anti-bullying programs in schools in curtailing the problem.

19. Do parents have a role in stopping the proliferation of bullying in schools? Explain.

20. What lasting impact can bullying have on a child? Explain.

5. Cyberbullying

1. What are some of the different forms of cyberbullying which occur on the Internet?
2. Describe the role that social media plays in regards to cyberbullying.
3. How does online anonymity further exacerbate cyberbullying and how it can be solved?
4. What are the main factors for the rise in cyberbullying among young people today?
5. Describe how some school deals with cyberbullying.
6. Is bullying in school less harmful than online bullying? Why or why not?
7. Explain how you could support a friend who is being cyberbullied. Cite examples.
8. Compare and contrast school bullying to cyberbullying? Which is worse?
9. What role can parents play in the prevention of cyberbullying?
10. What are the main reasons that children cyberbully their peers?
11. What are some intervention and prevention strategies that schools could implement to put a stop to cyberbullying?
12. Are the strategies that have been put in place to prevent cyberbullying effective? Explain.

13. Does the government have a role in stopping cyberbullying? If so, what? If not, why?

14. Describe some ways to increase awareness about cyberbullying among teenagers?

15. Describe an experience you had with cyberbullying.

16. How might cyberbullying evolve in the coming years?

17. What role should teachers play in preventing cyberbullying? Explain.

18. Should teenagers who are being cyberbullied outside of school, go to their parents, handle it on their own, or go to their teachers? Why?

19. Discuss the reasons why some teenagers prefer to handle cyberbullying on their own versus going to their teachers or parents.

20. Do you think that going to the police is an appropriate response to cyberbullying? Why or why not?

6. Education and Learning

1. What are the qualities and characteristics of a good teacher?
2. What makes a good student?
3. Should students be allowed to grade their teachers? Why or why not?
4. Are students being given too much homework nowadays?
5. Should corporal punishment be allowed in schools? Why or why not?
6. What is the impact of poverty on the educational outcome of students?
7. To what extent does social class affect the quality of education a student receives?
8. From the point of view of a student, what are the pros and cons of standardized tests in schools?
9. Compare and contrast private schools versus public schools.
10. What can schools do to promote and protect the rights of minority students? Explain.
11. How big a problem is bullying in your school? Explain.
12. What are some of the possible benefits of homeschooling versus public schools?
13. To what extent should students be punished for plagiarism?

14. Are small classes class sizes better than large ones? Why or why not?
15. Should schools be able to put tracking chips in ID cards of their students? Why, or why not?
16. How early is too early for children to start school? Why?
17. To what extent does culture play a part in education?
18. Is a college education necessary to be successful in life? Why or why not?
19. Other than the obvious, how does online learning differ from face to face learning?
20. Are subjects such as gym a waste of time? Why or why not?

7. Romeo and Juliet

1. Romeo and Juliet fell in love, at first sight. Do you believe that the concept of love, at first sight, is possible, or do you think it is merely a romantic fantasy? Explain why you feel this way.
2. If Romeo and Juliet hadn't met their untimely deaths, how do you think the story could have been ended? Do you think their union could have brought the Capulets and Montagues together or would it have only fueled their long going feud?
3. Choose another couple, besides Rome and Juliet, who were also 'star-crossed lovers.' Compare and contrast how the two relationships are different.
4. From the beginning of this play, you are told that Romeo and Juliet are victims of fate, star-crossed lovers whose deaths are unavoidable. Do you agree with the statement? Use the situations of the play and the characters, to prove or disprove the statement.
5. If you were a character in the story, and you were good friends with Romeo, how would you convince him not to take the poison and die for his lover? Do you believe your words would succeed? Could you have saved him? Why or why not?
6. Describe Romeo and Juliet's rebelliousness towards their parents. Compare and contrast that to modern-day rebellion.
7. Who do you believe is ultimately to blame for the deaths of Romeo and Juliet? Explain why.
8. Do you feel that Romeo's love of Rosalie weakens the credibility of the love he later had for Juliet? Give examples.

9. Were Romeo and Juliet really in love? Romeo only first caught sight of Juliet about an hour or two before they decided to get married; they had only spoken for at most ten minutes. Was their love as Juliet said, "too rash, too unadvised, too sudden"?

10. What other tragic elements are there in the play besides the fate of the hero and heroine?

11. If Romeo and Juliet had lived, do you think they would have anything to offer each other once the initial burst of passion calmed down? Would Romeo move on from Juliet as quickly as he moved on from Rosaline?

12. Is it all the fault of the Nurse and Friar? The Prince announces that "some shall be pardoned and some punished." Do either the Nurse or the Friar deserve punishment? Who else, in your opinion, might bear some responsibility for the two lovers' deaths?

13. Why do you think Romeo and Juliet is still such a masterpiece today? What qualities of the play still resonate with people in this day and age?

14. What last words do you think Romeo and Juliet would have wanted to say to their parents if they were given the chance?! What things do you think were necessary to convey but left unsaid between them?

15. What would Romeo and Juliet be like today? How do you imagine they would dress? What would their mannerisms be? What differences could their parents have the keep them apart?

16. Is it glorious or foolish, to die for love? Explain why?

17. Who would you consider to be the best "role model" in Romeo and Juliet? Explain why.

18. Do you think Romeo's love for Juliet could have faded with time? Why or why not? Use examples from the play.

19. If Romeo and Juliet were a historically accurate event, and you were a time travel traveler, what one event would you change that might change the course of the story and possibly prevent their untimely deaths?

20. If Romeo and Juliet were modern teenagers, they would be unlikely to turn to a monk and a nurse for advice/help. Who do you think their modern mentors be and why?

8. Harry Potter

1. Which is better, the book or the movie? Why?
2. Which character would you like to see developed further? Why?
3. Describe a few instances where foreshadowing is used.
4. Describe a time in the series when Harry Potter doesn't behave like a hero.
5. Discuss the death of Harry's parents and how the book showcases the bond between parent and child.
6. How is Harry Potter first introduced in the story? Explain.
7. Discuss one of the main problems in one of the books.
8. If you could choose one of the animals in the series to be your pet, which would it be? Why?
9. Who is the evilest character? Why?
10. Who is the real hero of the series? Why?
11. Is there a clear sense of good and evil in the series? Explain.
12. What's moral of the story? Explain.
13. What, in your opinion, do you think are the reasons for Harry Potter's success?
14. What is the significance of Harry Potter's scar?
15. Write a critical analysis of Professor Severus Snape, who appears in all the series.

16. How do some of the names of characters give us a clue about their personalities?
17. Reset the ending of the story. How would you change it? Why?
18. What are some of the common themes that run throughout the books?
19. What do you think will happen in future books?
20. Some people say that the series promote magic and witchcraft. Is there any truth to this? Explain.

9. The Hunger Games

1. What is the conflict in the story? Describe it.
2. What is the climax of the story? Explain it.
3. Which is better, the book or the movie? Why?
4. Which character do you relate to the most? Explain.
5. Which character would you like to see developed further? Why?
6. Were there any scenes in the story that you particularly liked? Why?
7. What makes Rue and Katniss trust each other and become partners? Discuss the relationship.
8. What major events in the story lead to Katniss's character development?
9. Why is the Capitol so powerful? Explain.
10. What are Katniss's hopes and dreams?
11. Are there any heroes in the story? Who? Why?
12. Is Katniss a strong main character? How do you feel about her? Why?
13. What's moral of the story? Explain.
14. What, in your opinion, do you think are the reasons for The Hunger Game's success?
15. Are you on Team Peeta or Team Gale? Why?

16. How does one's family background, class, or occupation change the way someone sees the world?

17. How would you change the ending of the story? Why?

18. Would you recommend this novel/movie to a friend? Do you want to read/watch the sequels?

19. What do you think will happen in future books?

20. Discuss the process of the Reaping. What is it, why does it take place, and how does it affect the districts?

10. Family & Childhood

1. What does family mean to you, and how has it shaped you? Explain.
2. How do you define family, and what does it mean to you to have a family? Explain.
3. How has the family evolved over the years? Discuss.
4. Evaluate and analyze your place in your family.
5. To what extent does technology affect family life? Cite examples.
6. What are some of your family's most important traditions?
7. Describe an unusual family tradition that your family engages in together.
8. What are some ways that religion affects your family life?
9. Discuss the most meaningful gift you've ever received from one of your family members.
10. Discuss a family member outside of your parents who have had the most influence on your life.
11. Describe a time you were embarrassed by something your parents did.
12. How has the parent-child relationship changed over time?
13. Describe an interesting person in your family.
14. What are some of the most important values of your family? Cite examples.

15. Describe your most poignant childhood memory.
16. Is a child that has been raised by one parent at a disadvantage over a child who was raised by both parents? Why, or why not?
17. What are some things about your current life that make you nostalgic about your childhood?
18. Which family member has had the most impact on your beliefs system? Explain.
19. Which family traditions do you think you will continue to do with your own children? Why?
20. Should both parents have equal authority in the family? Or should one parent have more influence than the other? If so, which one? If not, why?

11. Marriage and Divorce

1. Detail some of the adverse effects of divorce on children and teenagers.
2. What impact does divorce have on the emotional wellbeing of adolescents?
3. What are some ways that a family can cope with a divorce?
4. Is divorce harder on the parents or on the children? Why?
5. How does divorce impact a teenager's future relationships as they grow into adulthood?
6. What are some of the economic effects of divorce on a family?
7. Who should a child live with after a divorce, the mother or the father? Why?
8. Are arranged marriages better? Why?
9. Is it better to stay single or to marry? Why?
10. Who causes more arguments in a marriage? Men or Women? Why?
11. Are there any problems inherent in interracial marriages? Explain.
12. Are there any problems inherent in inter-faith marriages? Explain.
13. What are some of the advantages and disadvantages of interracial marriages?
14. Detail the advantages and disadvantages of marrying someone from a different faith?

15. At what age should young people be allowed to marry? Explain.
16. What is the most essential factor in choosing a spouse?
17. How important is it to get your parents' approval before getting married?
18. What, in your opinion, are the most important elements of a successful marriage?
19. Should a couple that is in an unhealthy relationship, stay in the union for the "children's sake?" Why or why not?
20. Is love the most crucial factor when choosing a spouse?
21. Are couples who live together before marriage at a higher risk of divorce? Why or why not?

12. Music

1. What genre of music appeals to you? Why?
2. What role has music played in shaping your life?
3. Why does music have such an impact on today's young people?
4. How does hip-hop influence your life or the life of your friends?
5. What are some positive and negative effects of music on today's youth?
6. If you could be adept at playing any musical instrument, which one would it be? Why?
7. Who, in your opinion, is the greatest musician of all time? Why?
8. Who, in your opinion, is the greatest singer of all time? Why?
9. What musician today should be a superstar, but is not?
10. How does country music differ from other types of music?
11. Music often conjures up emotions in people. Which song evokes memories of a special time in your life? Why?
12. Some songs or music are considered ageless. In your opinion, what song or music do you consider timeless? Explain why.
13. Which contemporary musician do you think will stand the test of time?
14. Compare and contrast popular music of the 1980s to popular music of the 2000s. What are the similarities and differences?

15. Are today's piracy laws adequate at curtailing illegal downloading and distribution of copyrighted music? Why or why not?

16. How has the music industry evolved since illegal downloading and distribution of copyrighted material has taken place?

17. Write a critical review of your favorite album. Provide an analysis of its strengths and weaknesses.

18. Describe a concert that you attended. What concert was it? Who went with you? Why has it stuck with you this long?

19. Compare and contrast the genre of music which you like the most to the one you like the least.

20. Why have some musicians been able to maintain success across generations in contrast to others who have come and gone?

13. TV, Celebrities & Movies

1. Who is your favorite celebrity – past or present? Why?
2. Should fans be privy to the private lives of celebrities? Why or why not?
3. Who would you like to have as a celebrity neighbor? Why?
4. Which celebrity are you obsessed with? Why?
5. If you could be the child of a star, who would it be? Why?
6. Are the benefits of being a celebrity, worth the loss of privacy? Explain.
7. Which reality show would you like to be a part of? Why?
8. What role does TV play in your life? Explain.
9. What's your favorite TV show? Why?
10. What's your favorite movie? Explain.
11. What are the qualities of a good film?
12. What stereotypes does reality TV perpetuate?
13. If you could turn a book you've read into a movie, which book would it be? Why?
14. What's the funniest TV show on television today? Explain.
15. What's the best movie you've seen this year? Discuss.
16. In what ways do TV and movies glamorize violence?

17. To what extent do you think you're influenced by TV and movies?
18. What is your favorite cartoon? Why?
19. Compare and contrast two of your favorite movies.
20. Which TV show do you think h the most detrimental effect on teenagers today? Why?

14. Sports (General)

1. How do students in high school benefit from being in sports? Cite examples.
2. What effect do sports have on the physical and emotional development of teenagers?
3. Should sports teams be coed? Why or why not?
4. How has sportsmanship behavior changed over time?
5. Are professional athletes overpaid? Why or why not?
6. Should there be a salary cap on the salaries of professional athletes?
7. How should doping be handled in professional sports?
8. Should steroids in sports be legalized? Why or why not?
9. Should a player be banned from a team for doing drugs? Explain.
10. Does taking steroids give some athletes an unfair advantage? Why or why not?
11. Who, in your opinion, is the best basketball player of all time? Discuss your choice.
12. Who, in your opinion, is the best football player of all time? Explain.
13. Compare and contrast the careers of two of your favorite basketball players.

14. Compare and contrast the careers of two of your favorite tennis players.

15. Write a critical review of your favorite sports team.

16. Should athletes be allowed to "take the knee" during the national anthem? Why or why not?

17. Given that so many young people look up to athletes, should athletes be held to a higher standard of behavior? Why or why not?

18. Should extreme sports be banned? Why or why not?

19. Should animal sports such as bullfighting be illegal? Why or why not?

20. Should sports betting be legalized? Explain.

15. Basketball

1. What aspects do you like most about basketball? Why?
2. Which conference do you like better, the East or the West? Explain why.
3. If you could be a professional basketball player, which position would you play? Why?
4. Who do you think is the better player in the game today, Lebron James or Kevin Durant? Why?
5. Which team was the greatest in the history of basketball? Why?
6. Which one year's team (for example The 2009 Boston Celtics) was the strongest you've ever seen (or read about)?
7. Describe your first experience of going to a basketball game.
8. Describe the most exciting game you ever saw.
9. Who do you think was the most dominant basketball player of all time? Why?
10. Since the 3-point shot is a lower percentage shot but worth more points, explain why you think it is a good strategy for a team to shoot many 3 pointers, or why you think it is a bad strategy.
11. If you had a team and could choose either James Harden, Steph Curry, or Kawhi Leonard, who would you choose? Explain why you would choose him over the other two players.

12. Would you rather your team have a strong defense or a strong offense? Explain why you think one is more important than the other.

13. Who do you think will win the NBA Championship next year? Why?

14. If you could select an All-Star team, who would you pick for each position? Why?

15. If your team was losing by 2 points with 7 seconds to play, describe a smart play you could use to help your team either tie the game up or win it. Why do you think your play would work?

16. What do you think is the most important position in basketball? Why?

17. What is your favorite position to play? Why?

18. Describe your best game ever as a player.

19. Compare and contrast a great player of the past with a player of the present.

20. How would you describe the game of basketball to someone who has never heard of the sport?

16. Baseball

1. What is your favorite baseball team? Why?
2. Who is your favorite baseball player? Why?
3. Compare and contrast your two favorite baseball teams.
4. Compare and contrast your two favorite baseball players.
5. What do you think is more important? Hitting for power, or hitting for average? Why?
6. Which team was the greatest in the history of the sport? Why?
7. Which player has had the greatest influence on the sport?
8. Describe your first experience of going to a baseball game.
9. Describe the most exciting game you ever saw.
10. Who do you think was the greatest player of all time? Why?
11. Who do you think is the best pitcher of all time? Why?
12. Who do you think is the best pitcher today? Why?
13. Mariano Rivera was the first player to be voted into the Hall of Fame unanimously. Who do you think will be next?
14. Who do you think will win the World Series this year? Why?
15. If you could select an Allstar team, who would you pick for each position? Why?
16. What are the qualities that make someone a good manager in baseball?

17. What do you think is the most important position in baseball? Why?
18. What is your favorite position to play? Why?
19. Describe your best game ever as a player?
20. Compare and contrast a player of the past with a player of the present.

17. Football

1. What's your favorite football team? Why?
2. Who is your favorite football player? Why?
3. Compare and contrast your two favorite football players.
4. Compare and contrast the two teams that you think are the strongest teams in football.
5. Which conference do you think is the strongest? The NFC or the AFC? Why?
6. Which do you think is important? Having a strong running game or a strong passing game? Why?
7. Who do you think is the best quarterback in the game today? Why?
8. Who do you think is the greatest quarterback of the past? Why?
9. Discuss what make-up a strong defense?
10. If you could meet your favorite football player of all time, what
11. Is football considered too dangerous for teenagers today? Why or why not?
12. Compare and contrast the dangers of football to the risks of boxing?
13. Imagine an alien just came to earth and has no idea what football is. Describe the game to them.
14. Which football players would you include in your dream team? Why?

15. Explain who you think is the best running back in the game. Why?
16. Who do you think will win the Super Bowl this year? Why?
17. Explain which player you think has had the most impact on the game? Why?
18. Do you think football players should be allowed to kneel during the national anthem? Why or why not?
19. If you were a player on your favorite team, would you play offence or defense? Why?
20. Describe the greatest game-winning play you ever saw.

18. Politics

1. Do you feel patriotic about the country? Why or why not?
2. What benefits do citizens gain from their governments?
3. How do you think about our current political system? Explain.
4. Who is the politician you most identify with presently? Why?
5. What is your political leaning? How did you develop your viewpoint?
6. Should we interpret the laws of the country the way the founding fathers intended, or should they be interpreted according to current circumstances? Explain.
7. Should there be strict limits on campaign spending or should anyone be able to donate whatever they want? Why or why not?
8. How does the political process in the United States compare to other countries? Explain.
9. If you were running for political office, what would your platform be? Explain.
10. Should the United States have more than two political parties? Why or why not?
11. Do political ads influence the way you think? Explain.
12. Should everyone pay the same in taxes? Why or why not?
13. Should the rich pay more in taxes? Explain.

14. Should supreme court justices have lifetime appointments? Why or why not?
15. Would you consider running for office? Why or why not?
16. Should ordinary citizens be able to own assault weapons? Explain.
17. Should ordinary citizens be able to own guns? Explain.
18. If you could change anything about the current political system, what would it be?
19. Would you demonstrate or march for something you believe? Why or why not?
20. Should citizens be required to show identification before they're allowed to vote? Explain your point of view.

19. Nonfiction

1. Detail a "twist of faith" that occurred in your life.
2. Discuss a long-term goal that you've accomplished.
3. Describe a time when you felt like a "fish out to water."
4. Write about a time you had to deal with a catastrophe in your family.
5. Write a critical review of your favorite book.
6. Write about a time you had a belief fundamentally shaken.
7. What's something you'd like to change most about your life? Why?
8. What is something you'd like to be remembered for? Explain.
9. In what ways are you affected by peer pressure? Cite examples.
10. Describe a moment in your life you'd like to re-live.
11. Describe a moment in your life you'd rather forget.
12. Describe a time someone came into your life and left a lasting impact.
13. Detail your greatest character strength. How did you discover it?
14. Detail your greatest character flaw. How did you find out it? How will you try to improve it?
15. Write about a current event that concerns you.
16. Detail a cause that you're passionate about. Why are you excited about it?

17. If you could meet a famous person, who would it be? Why? What would you want to talk to them about?
18. Describe a career you'd like to have. Why?
19. Detail some challenges or obstacles you've had to overcome in your life. Cite examples.
20. Describe an experience that has changed the way you look at life.

20. Narrative Writing

1. Write about a single father who is a superhero.
2. Write about a homeless man who wins the lottery.
3. Write about a teenager who becomes homeless.
4. Write about a couple that work as a private investigator duo.
5. Write about a teenager who spends 24 hours with his favorite sports hero.
6. Write about a 90-year-old man with the memory of a 20-year-old.
7. Write about two people who dream about each other before they switch places.
8. Write about two pirates who discover a mountain of fool's gold.
9. Write about a billionaire who has no heir.
10. Write about a group of evil scientists who are trying to rule the world.
11. Write about a teenager who can read the minds of his teachers.
12. Write about two twins who were adopted by separate families at birth.
13. Write about a mad scientist who invents a time machine.
14. Write about a blind man who suddenly gains his sight back.
15. Write about a poor boy who grows up to be king.
16. Write about an undercover spy who gets caught.

17. Write about a mermaid who dreams of being human.

18. Write about a teenager who hitchhikes across the country to meet his hero.

19. Write about a teenager with a special power.

20. Write about a girl who can't lie even to save her life.

21. Expository Writing

1. Describe a public health concern that you think deserves immediate action.
2. Discuss how instant fame and fortune can change a person's life.
3. Describe some techniques and strategies that could help people stop smoking.
4. Explain the causes that lead teenagers to smoke
5. Explain why some teens do drugs.
6. Describe the consequences of doing drugs.
7. Explain what diversity means to you.
8. Explain the cause and effect of a poor diet.
9. Describe your vision of an ideal world.
10. Explain why some teens join gangs.
11. Explain the impact of Bulimia
12. Describe the effects of Anorexia.
13. Discuss what leads some teens to eating disorders.
14. Describe your favorite digital game and explain why you like it.
15. Describe how weather affects your mood.
16. Explain why you're a vegetarian.
17. Explain why you think you could never be a vegetarian.

18. Describe a typical day in your life.

19. Discuss the chores and responsibilities that you have at home.

20. Explain the reasoning behind some teens getting part-time jobs.

22. Creative Writing Story Starters

1. Sean knew that he only had one shot at winning.
2. "Stop wasting your life with him," my mother said.
3. I opened it up, and scrawled inside were the words: "the future of the world is in your hands."
4. Today is the day I'll find out who I really am.
5. The whole class laughed when Megan got up to speak.
6. I got up to the podium, and I could hear a pin drop.
7. "Hey, you!" The words stopped me in my tracks. I couldn't believe I was caught.
8. As he looked into the distance, what he saw shocked him.
9. My sister was changing; there was no question about that. The problem was, why?
10. In a panic she ran out the door, dropping her wallet on the floor.
11. It was the last time they would ever see each other again.
12. Trembling, I took his hand and led him down the corridor to the room on the left.
13. His secret hiding place had been ransacked!
14. It was her worst hair day, and now this had to happen!
15. He missed his flight, and now there was only one person he could turn to.

16. The writing on the envelope was faded. It looked like it could have been written 50 years ago.

17. She picked up the wallet and slipped it into his bag. She was sure no one saw her do it.

18. It was the happiest day of my life. I couldn't believe my dream had finally come true after all so many failures.

19. He looked at me with cold blue eyes and said, "I don't believe you, Jessica."

20. Suddenly she woke up, unaware of where she was.

23. Out of the Box

1. Describe your favorite teacher.
2. Describe the life of your favorite athlete.
3. Describe the life of your favorite celebrity.
4. Discuss a part-time job that you'd like to have.
5. If you could go on a dream vacation anywhere in the world, would it be?
6. What is your greatest wish for yourself?
7. Imagine your life as a book. Write a review for it.
8. What is your most vivid childhood memory? Explain.
9. Write about a fear.
10. Write about a regret.
11. Write about your worst day at school. Explain what made it the worst.
12. Write about your best day at school. Explain what made it the best.
13. What bad habits do you struggle with the most? Cite examples.
14. Do you believe people should get second chances? Why or why not?
15. Discuss a time when someone gave you a second chance? What happened? How did it make you feel?
16. Are anti-smoking campaigns effective deterrent for teenagers?

17. Would you consider becoming a vegetarian? Why or why not?

18. Write about going back to school after summer vacation.

19. Are the Oscars too white? Why or why not?

20. Is it harder being a girl or a boy? Why?

24. Would you Rather

1. Would you rather cry at the drop of a hat or never find anything funny? Explain.
2. Would you rather be hated or be feared? Why?
3. Would you rather disappoint your parents or have your parents disappoint you? Why?
4. Would you rather break someone's heart or have your heart broken? Why?
5. Would you rather have a class that doesn't give homework or one that doesn't give tests? Explain.
6. Would you rather be the best athlete in school or the homecoming king/queen? Why?
7. Would you rather be the most popular student in school or the smartest? Why?
8. Would you rather solve world hunger or solve world racism? Why?
9. Would you rather go to prom alone or stay home? Justify your choice.
10. Would you rather have no sense of smell or no sense of taste? Explain.
11. Would you rather have x-ray vision or the ability to be invisible? Justify your answer.

12. Would you rather read people's minds or control how people think? Why?
13. Would you rather have a 2-day vacation somewhere exciting or a one-week "staycation" at home? Explain.
14. Would you rather die happy at 100 years old or get reborn every 20 years forever? Justify your answer.
15. Would you rather get up early or stay up late? Explain.
16. Would you rather win $1,000 which you can spend on yourself or have your family win $10,000 which will probably go to pay bills? Why?
17. Would you rather vacation with your friends or with your family? Explain.
18. Would you rather eat Chinese food for every meal or Italian food for every meal? Why?
19. Would you rather live in a haunted house or have nightmares every night? Why?
20. Would you rather be the teacher or the student? Explain.

25. Lists

1. Write a detailed list of the top goals you'd like to accomplish in your life and explain the importance of each one.
2. Write a detailed list of 20 things you're grateful for and explain each one.
3. Write a list of your favorite childhood memories.
4. Write a detailed list of 20 places you'd like to visit in the future and explain why you'd like to visit them.
5. Write a list of 20 of your favorite quotes. Tell why they're a favorite.
6. Write a detailed list describing some of your firsts. i.e., your first kiss, your first job, etc.
7. Write a detailed bucket list of 20 things you'd like to do.
8. Write a detailed list of the top things that make you happy and explain why they make you happy.
9. Write a detailed description of your favorite activities.
10. Write a detailed list of people you admire and explain why you admire them.
11. Write a detailed list of things you've never done, but would like to do.
12. Write a list of 20 things you're looking forward to in your life as an adult.

13. Write a detailed description of your pet peeves.
14. Write a list of business ideas you could do with your interests and talents.
15. Write a detailed list of the best advice you've gotten over the years.
16. Write a detailed list of funny things that have happened to you.
17. Write a detailed list of things you'd buy if you suddenly became a millionaire.
18. Write a detailed list of questions you'd like to ask your favorite author.
19. Write a detailed list of questions you'd like to ask your favorite celebrity.
20. Write a detailed list describing your favorite games.

Made in United States
Orlando, FL
27 August 2023